Franziska Kracht

Dynamics between Culture and Commerce in Media Globalisation Debates

GRIN Verlag

Bibliografische Information der Deutschen Nationalbibliothek:

Die Deutsche Bibliothek verzeichnet diese Publikation in der Deutschen National-
bibliografie; detaillierte bibliografische Daten sind im Internet über http://dnb.d-
nb.de/ abrufbar.

Imprint:

Copyright © 2010 GRIN Verlag GmbH
Druck und Bindung: Books on Demand GmbH, Norderstedt Germany
ISBN: 978-3-656-46610-9

This book at GRIN:

http://www.grin.com/en/e-book/230452/dynamics-between-culture-and-commerce-
in-media-globalisation-debates

GRIN - Your knowledge has value

Der GRIN Verlag publiziert seit 1998 wissenschaftliche Arbeiten von Studenten, Hochschullehrern und anderen Akademikern als eBook und gedrucktes Buch. Die Verlagswebsite www.grin.com ist die ideale Plattform zur Veröffentlichung von Hausarbeiten, Abschlussarbeiten, wissenschaftlichen Aufsätzen, Dissertationen und Fachbüchern.

Visit us on the internet:

http://www.grin.com/

http://www.facebook.com/grincom

http://www.twitter.com/grin_com

Question 2 Final Media Essay:

Critically discuss the dynamics between culture and commerce in media globalisation debates.

Use relevant examples to justify and elaborate your arguments.

1. Introduction

Globalisation and its consequences on local culture are one of the most addressed academic issues since the mid- 80s (Durham & Kellner, 2006, p. 579). Media globalisation debates play an important role in this since the media are increasingly shaping cultures.

In popular discourse media globalisation is often associated with the loss of the local media culture, i.e. homogenisation as well as with terms such as Americanisation, Westernization etc. The import of American content to local media usually presents the main thread to local culture. Having a closer look at the Australian film industry this essay demonstrates the dynamics between the culture versus commerce argument via Australian media globalisation debates and its outcomes.

2. Media globalisation debates and the culture versus commerce arguments

The fear of Americanisation is often present in media globalisation debates. It includes the vast intensity of American media, their brands, industrial and consumption models. Pessimists state this process to be overwhelming, transforming the local media culture into the American (Hamelink, 1983). This is seen as especially concerning since American content is seen as mindless commerce whereas the local content is mostly regarded as culture delivering a cultivating message.

Having a closer look at film industries the overwhelming presence as well as popularity of American movies in foreign countries cannot be denied.

In 2009 in Australia nine out of ten top ten profitable movies were American, none were of Australian origin, although Australia released 38 Australian movies in the same year (Australian film institute 2010) (boxoffice mojo 2010). In the Top 30 of the most successful movies of all times except for a few exceptions of Harry Potter and Lord of the rings every movie is off American origin.

Hollywood is very influential since it is no longer just a place, but also a brand. Film studios own films, market themselves etc. They are powerful brands that are associated with a promised film experience. People can rely on these brands and will go and watch their movies. More powerful brands also mean more spending money. The average cost of a movie produced in Hollywood in 2006 was around 100.3 million US Dollars (Motion Picture Association of America) whereas the average film budget for Australian movies in 2005 was 3.7 million US Dollars (Screen Digest 2006). This comparison shows how much more powerful and influential the American movie sphere is compared to Australia. Looking at those numbers it is understandable how American movies are often classified as commercial since they are produced for a large audience, they are increasingly marketed. Hollywood is an industry, a business which produces for making blockbusters. They invest a lot but get a lot of money in return.

3. The contemporary Australian film industry

The Australian film industry however has a character very different from Hollywood. Similar to advertising and television content regulation, Australia also has specific regulation concerning the financing of films. Since the 1970s cultural policy has established and sustained the Australian film industry (Ryan 2009). The public funding bodies only fund films which foster the representation and preservation of Australian culture, character and identity (ibid). The Australian film commission, which was established in 1975, values quality and cultural content over entertainment and commercialism. Genre films are regarded as mindless commerce and are thus not funded whereas art house films emphasising Australianness and social realism shape the Australian film industry.

4. National identity

With this policy Australia is clearly distinguishing itself from Hollywood content. By having such a strict policy Australia is trying to deliver a certain image of national identity. Setting those restrictions to Australian filmmakers that only deliver a certain image of Australia can be seen as an effect of the long struggle the country has had to establish a national identity. Scholars argue that Australia might be the country which has most troubles creating a national identity in the world. The media are an important way in which nation building (Benedict Anderson) functions, which is reflected in Australia's film industry.

5. Effects of Australia's cultural policy on the film industry

Ryan notes that the cultural policy has clearly had positive impacts for Australian culture altogether, facilitating a large volume of cultural expression contributing to a sense of national identity. It is also clearly positive that bodies like the Australian film commission and the just recently established Screen support cultural content, distinctive stories and so on rather than just seeing the economic value of films. It is good to know that people still support art. But there are not only positive effects of the Australian cultural policy on the industry.

As Verhoeven argues, the number of the audience who is watching Australian art house films is considerably declining whereas the total number of audiences is increasing. As the Top profitable movies have demonstrated, the Hollywood genre films are generally simply more popular in the population. This indicates a need to rethink the narrow cultural policy. Who is Australia making movies for? Furthermore if the movies are not profitable enough the amount of funding available will shrink increasingly, making it hard for filmmakers to produce their art. As Hollywood has shown they have a lot of budget, which does not necessarily mean better movies but it definitely makes it easier and gives the opportunity for filmmakers to create something high quality, which is in the "public interest".

In an era of media globalisation creating something purely "Australian", which stabilises the Australian national identity also becomes increasingly difficult. The film sector becomes more and more integrated into a global audiovisual sector, which constitutes the Australian content to blur. Who even decides what is Australian content and which is not in a multi-cultural society? As the following example shows, the Australian content simply has to work in favour of the national identity which is aimed to be produced.

The art-house film *Piano* was directed by a New Zealander and shot in New Zealand but financed by Australian public finance. It was celebrated as being Australian. However *Dark City* was written and directed by an Australian but financed by an international studio and consequently not considered Australian.

National cinema is an approach which needs reconsideration as real growth is occurring across national boundaries due to globalisation.

By examining the genre of horror films Ryan also exemplifies some other issues which the narrow cultural policy brings up. Ryan argues that Australian horror films, although most of them haven't received any fundings from the Australian government have been a greater national and international success than arthouse films. He even states that Australian horror has developed a brand which is internationally known and appreciated. However, as most films don't receive any funding because they are considered to be genre films, many filmmakers and their movies go abroad. The *Saw franchise* has become the most successful horror franchise of all time and was created by Australian filmmakers. However the production went overseas since the Australian filmmakers did not receive any subventions.

Ryan argues that Australia has created some great horror films, which are cost efficient to produce, which have established a brand and which are a genre in which many young filmmakers start their production.

Furthermore young filmmakers who have been influenced with genre films and now want to tell "their own stories" do not get the opportunity to do so in Australia. As *Saw* as well as successful filmmaker such as Colin Eggleston, who moved abroad in order to be able to produce films they wanted to produce show, Australia's cultural policy drives away good filmmakers.